The Housemaid (2025)

Inside the Dark Psychology, Hidden Secrets, and Shocking Twists of the Film Starring Sydney Sweeney, Amanda Seyfried, Brandon Sklenar, Michele Morrone, and Elizabeth Perkins

Kate Cindel

Copyright

All rights reserved. No part of this book may be reproduced, stored in a retrieval system, or transmitted in any form or by any means, electronic, mechanical, photocopying, recording, or otherwise, without the prior written permission of the publisher, except for brief quotations used in reviews.

This book is a work of nonfiction. Any similarity to real persons, living or dead, is coincidental and not intended by the author.

© 2025 by Kate Cindel

Disclaimer

This book is an independent work of nonfiction analysis and commentary created for educational, critical, and informational purposes. It is not affiliated with, authorized by, endorsed by, or produced in association with the filmmakers, production companies, distributors, studios, or any individuals involved in the creation of The Housemaid (2025).

The Housemaid (2025) and all related names, characters, likenesses, and titles are the property of their respective copyright and trademark holders and are referenced in this book under principles of fair use for the purposes of critique, commentary, and analysis.

The content of this book reflects interpretive analysis of the film's themes, psychology, narrative structure, and cultural context. Any psychological, sociological, or thematic interpretations presented are offered as critical perspectives and should not be construed as factual assertions about the real-life beliefs, intentions, or personal conduct of the actors, filmmakers, or creative contributors.

This book does not claim to present official explanations, behind-the-scenes accounts, or definitive interpretations of the film. Any dates, cultural references, or contextual discussions are included to support analytical commentary and do not imply direct confirmation or endorsement by the film's creators.

This work is not intended to provide medical, psychological, legal, or professional advice. Readers experiencing distress related to themes discussed in this book are encouraged to seek support from qualified professionals.

All opinions expressed are those of the author alone and are intended to promote thoughtful discussion and deeper understanding of the film's narrative and psychological impact.

Table of Contents

Introduction	7
Chapter One	20
Welcome to the Perfect House	20
Chapter Two	**33**
Millie Calloway — A Past That Never Stays Buried	33
Chapter Three	47
Nina Winchester — Charm, Volatility, and Control	47
Chapter Four	**62**
The Winchester House as a Psychological Trap	62
Chapter Five	**78**
Andrew Winchester — Savior, Bystander, or Architect	78
Chapter Six	91
Class, Wealth, and Invisible Power	91
Chapter Seven	104
Enzo and the Illusion of Escape	104
Chapter Eight	**118**
Gaslighting as a Weapon	118
Chapter Nine	**133**
Secrets Behind the Smiles	133
Chapter Ten	**146**
The Twists That Change Everything	146
Chapter Eleven	**158**
The Final Act — Justice, Revenge, or Survival	158

Chapter Twelve   **172**
    Why The Housemaid Gets Under Your Skin 172

Introduction

"People don't fear monsters in the dark nearly as much as they fear the moment they realize they've been living with one." That idea sits quietly at the center of *The Housemaid (2025)*, a film released in December 2025 that arrived not as a loud shock machine but as a slow, suffocating psychological pressure test. Adapted from Freida McFadden's 2022 novel, the film did not depend on elaborate spectacle or overt violence to unsettle its audience. Instead, it worked through implication, imbalance, and the quiet terror of dependence. What makes the story linger is not simply what happens, but how easily it could happen—and how familiar its emotional mechanics feel in a world where power often hides behind politeness, wealth, and curated appearances.

By the time *The Housemaid* reached theaters in late 2025, audiences were already steeped in domestic thrillers, stories centered on homes that become cages and relationships that turn predatory behind closed doors. Yet this film distinguished itself by refusing to rush its revelations. It demanded patience, forcing viewers to sit inside discomfort rather than sprint toward resolution. The tension grows from small humiliations, from glances held too long, from rules that are never written down but are enforced all the same. The Winchester house does not feel dangerous at first glance. It feels aspirational. Clean lines, manicured spaces, wealth that signals safety. That contrast is deliberate. The film understands that the most effective control is exercised where resistance seems unreasonable.

This book is designed to slow the experience down even further, to examine what the film implies rather than simply what it shows. The goal is not to retell the story beat by beat, but to understand the psychological scaffolding holding it together. Every character operates within a system of incentives and fears shaped by class, trauma, gender expectations, and the need to be believed. Those systems are rarely visible on the surface, but they determine who speaks freely, who stays silent, and who is punished for crossing invisible boundaries.

Millie Calloway's arrival in the Winchester household is the narrative's ignition point, but it is not its true origin. Her desperation is not accidental; it is cultivated by a society that offers second chances in theory while punishing those who need them most in practice. The film places her at the intersection of economic precarity and moral judgment, a position that strips her of credibility before she ever opens her mouth. This dynamic reflects a broader truth supported by social research long before the film's release: individuals with criminal records face systemic barriers to housing and employment years after completing their sentences, a reality documented repeatedly in studies throughout the 2010s and early 2020s. By 2023, multiple U.S. labor reports confirmed that formerly incarcerated individuals were still far more likely to accept unsafe or exploitative work simply to survive. *The Housemaid* uses that reality as its foundation, not its background.

The structure of this book mirrors the film's

methodical tightening of control. Early chapters focus on orientation rather than accusation. They examine how normality is constructed, how authority is introduced gently, and how compliance is framed as gratitude. The Winchester household operates on unspoken hierarchies that are never formally explained to Millie, yet she is expected to understand them immediately. Mistakes are not treated as errors but as moral failures. Praise is given sparingly, criticism freely. These patterns are not accidental; they are textbook mechanisms of psychological dominance documented in studies of coercive control dating back decades, including work by psychologist Evan Stark in the early 2000s. The film translates those theories into lived experience, showing how domination does not require constant aggression, only consistency.

As the chapters progress, the analysis deepens into psychological warfare that is subtle enough to be deniable. Gaslighting is not portrayed as a dramatic event but as a process. Reality is adjusted incrementally. Memory is questioned casually. Emotional reactions are reframed as instability. By the mid-2010s, gaslighting had entered mainstream vocabulary, but *The Housemaid* demonstrates how the concept is still widely misunderstood. It is not about making someone believe something untrue all at once; it is about exhausting their confidence in their own perceptions over time. The film's release in 2025 felt particularly timely in a cultural moment shaped by misinformation, image curation, and competing versions of truth, where authority often belongs to those who appear calm, wealthy, and composed.

This book also examines the role of the physical environment in enforcing psychological control. The Winchester house is not merely a setting; it is an instrument. Locked rooms, surveillance-like awareness, and spatial isolation contribute to Millie's sense of being watched and evaluated at all times. Architectural psychology has long explored how space influences behavior, with research as early as the 1970s linking environmental design to stress, submission, and compliance. By the 2020s, those ideas were increasingly applied to discussions of domestic abuse and workplace exploitation. The film visualizes these concepts without naming them, trusting the audience to feel what the character feels rather than explaining it aloud.

The presence of Andrew Winchester complicates the narrative in ways that resist easy categorization. He is not overtly cruel, nor is he overtly protective. His ambiguity is precisely what makes him dangerous. This book treats that ambiguity seriously, examining how passivity can function as power when combined with status and silence. Sociological studies published between 2018 and 2024 repeatedly emphasized that harm is often sustained not by active cruelty alone, but by those who benefit from the system while claiming neutrality. Andrew's role invites readers to question how often comfort masquerades as innocence.

Secondary characters, including Enzo and the

extended family figures, serve as mirrors rather than solutions. They represent perceived exits that ultimately reinforce the same structures of control. The illusion of escape is as psychologically potent as captivity itself. Research into abusive dynamics has consistently shown that intermittent hope is one of the strongest tools of manipulation, a concept first formally identified in behavioral psychology through studies on variable reinforcement in the mid-20th century. The film adapts this principle into narrative form, offering moments of relief that ultimately deepen dependency.

What makes the twists of *The Housemaid* resonate is not their shock value, but their inevitability. By the time revelations arrive, the groundwork has been laid so thoroughly that the audience recognizes the logic even as they recoil from the outcome. This book approaches those twists not as surprises to be spoiled, but as psychological consequences. Power shifts, role reversals, and moral redefinitions do not emerge out of nowhere; they are the result of pressures applied steadily over time. Understanding that progression transforms the story from a thriller into a case study in survival psychology.

Culturally, the film arrived during a period when conversations about female rage, credibility, and institutional disbelief were gaining renewed attention. From high-profile legal cases in the early 2020s to broader discussions about emotional labor and domestic exploitation, audiences were primed to recognize the patterns the film depicts. *The Housemaid* does not offer catharsis through simple justice. Instead, it presents survival as an active, morally complex process. This book embraces that complexity rather than resolving it, allowing readers to sit with discomfort rather than escape it.

Each chapter that follows is designed to function independently while contributing to a cumulative understanding of the story's psychological weight. Characters are examined not as heroes or villains, but as products and agents of systems that reward silence, punish vulnerability, and disguise cruelty as refinement. The analysis draws connections between the film's fictional events and real-world dynamics documented across decades of psychological, sociological, and legal research. Dates, contexts, and cultural shifts are not included as decoration, but as anchors grounding the narrative in reality.

By approaching *The Housemaid* in this way, the book resists the temptation to flatten the story into entertainment alone. It treats the film as a reflection of how power operates in intimate spaces, how fear can be cultivated without threats, and how survival often requires strategies that blur traditional moral boundaries. What lingers after the screen goes dark is not simply the memory of twists, but the recognition of patterns that feel uncomfortably familiar. This introduction sets the stage for that exploration, not to explain everything at once, but to establish the lens through which every chapter should be read, leaving the unease intact rather than resolving it.

Chapter One

Welcome to the Perfect House

"By 2022, more than 60 percent of American workers reported living paycheck to paycheck, including nearly half of those earning over six figures." That statistic circulated widely in labor reports and financial journalism during the early 2020s, and it quietly frames the emotional reality that *The Housemaid (2025)* steps into from its very first moments. The film does not open with violence or shock. It opens with need. With the kind of need that feels ordinary, familiar, and socially invisible in the years following 2018, accelerating sharply after March 2020, when the pandemic fractured economic stability and turned employment into a source of fear rather than security.

The idea of "the perfect job offer" has long existed in thrillers, but in the post-pandemic era it takes on sharper edges. Between 2018 and 2025, job security eroded across sectors once considered stable. Service work, domestic labor, caregiving, and live-in arrangements expanded quietly as housing costs surged and wages failed to keep pace with inflation. By 2021, U.S. rental prices were climbing at their fastest rate in decades. By 2023, inflation had reshaped daily decision-making for millions. Against this backdrop, Millie's desperation in *The Housemaid* is not exaggerated; it is precise. She is not chasing luxury. She is chasing containment: a room, meals, routine, and the fragile promise that if she behaves correctly, life might stop unraveling.

The Winchester job arrives framed as benevolence. Live-in. Private space. Steady pay. Minimal questions. The film understands that in the early 2020s, generosity itself can feel suspicious, but also irresistible. When systems fail, individuals cling to lifelines even when they sense the rope may be frayed. Domestic thrillers exploit this tension by presenting opportunity as intimacy. You are not just hired. You are welcomed. You are folded into a household. That intimacy collapses professional boundaries, replacing contracts with gratitude, and rules with expectations that are never spoken aloud.

Millie's criminal past intensifies this dynamic. By the late 2010s, studies on post-incarceration employment showed that applicants with records were rejected at disproportionately high rates, even when qualified. By 2020, pandemic layoffs pushed formerly incarcerated individuals even further to the margins. In that climate, the Winchester offer is not merely attractive; it is improbable. The film lets this improbability hover without comment. There is no dramatic emphasis, no warning music cue. Instead, the danger is embedded in normalcy. In how easily the offer bypasses formal vetting. In how quickly the house replaces the world outside.

From its opening frames, the film uses pacing to signal unease while refusing to name it. Scenes breathe longer than expected. Conversations pause a beat too late. Dialogue is polite but oddly incomplete. Nina's warmth arrives with qualifiers, her smiles punctuated by abrupt tonal shifts that are easy to excuse as stress or eccentricity. Andrew's calmness feels reassuring precisely because it lacks emotional texture. The camera lingers on thresholds: doorways, staircases, hallways that recede into shadow. These choices do not announce threat; they suggest containment. The house does not loom. It encloses.

Domestic thrillers rely on a familiar psychological exchange: safety offered in exchange for silence. Between 2018 and 2025, this exchange became increasingly legible to audiences conditioned by precarious work, at-will employment, and the erosion of institutional protection. The Winchester home promises insulation from chaos outside, but it quietly demands compliance inside. Millie accepts without negotiation, not because she is naive, but because negotiation itself feels dangerous when one is disposable.

Her first day inside the house unfolds with a choreography of small signals that the film trusts viewers to feel before they understand. Nina's instructions are delivered casually, but not casually enough. There is precision beneath the friendliness. Certain spaces are shown but not entered. Certain routines are mentioned but not explained. The absence of clarity becomes its own form of guidance: do not ask too many questions. Silence functions as a test. Millie passes by adapting.

Psychological research between 2005 and 2020 repeatedly demonstrated how first impressions are shaped less by information than by power dynamics. Authority bias encourages individuals to defer judgment when the perceived cost of resistance is high. In Millie's case, the cost is homelessness, unemployment, exposure. The Winchesters do not need to threaten her. The structure does that work for them. Politeness becomes pressure. Hospitality becomes leverage.

The film mirrors this process in how it trains its audience. Early red flags are present, but they are framed as ambiguous. Nina's sharpness can be interpreted as moodiness. Andrew's distance can be mistaken for respect. The locked doors can be justified as privacy. The house's size can be admired rather than questioned. Viewers, like Millie, are encouraged to rationalize discomfort.

This alignment is deliberate. The film does not ask the audience to observe manipulation from a distance; it invites them to participate in it.

Body language carries much of this weight. Nina's eye contact holds just long enough to unsettle. Her movements through the house feel proprietary, territorial. Andrew positions himself as mediator without ever fully intervening, a pattern documented in studies on passive authority figures who maintain control by appearing neutral. Millie's posture shifts subtly as the day progresses. Shoulders tighten. Speech shortens. Compliance becomes automatic. These changes are not highlighted, but they accumulate.

Silence operates as the film's most effective warning system. Conversations trail off instead of ending. Questions go unanswered without explanation. The absence of correction creates uncertainty. In social psychology, this tactic has been associated with behavioral conditioning: individuals adapt to unspoken rules by overcorrecting their own behavior. Millie cleans more thoroughly than required. She apologizes preemptively. She absorbs blame without protest. The house rewards this with temporary calm.

Spatial cues reinforce hierarchy. Millie's room, though private, is physically removed from the heart of the house. It is functional, not inviting. The camera shows her learning the geography of the space cautiously, as though memorizing escape routes she does not yet know she will need. Doors are framed as boundaries rather than entrances. Light diminishes as one moves deeper into the house, a visual metaphor for the narrowing of autonomy.

By the early 2020s, discussions of workplace toxicity increasingly focused on subtle abuse rather than overt hostility. *The Housemaid* situates itself firmly within that discourse. The Winchesters do not raise their voices. They do not issue ultimatums. They rely on implication. This reflects real-world power dynamics documented in studies of coercive environments, where ambiguity is used to maintain control while preserving plausible deniability.

The film's restraint is what makes its opening so effective. It resists sensationalism. It allows viewers to sit in discomfort without resolution.

That discomfort is familiar to anyone who has accepted unfavorable conditions because the alternative felt worse. Between 2018 and 2025, millions made similar calculations: staying in unstable jobs, tolerating unsafe workplaces, remaining silent to avoid loss. The film taps into that collective experience without naming it.

Millie's internal rationalizations mirror those documented in trauma-informed research. She reframes unease as gratitude. She interprets cruelty as misunderstanding. She tells herself she is lucky. These narratives are not imposed by the Winchesters; they are adopted by Millie as survival strategies. The film's brilliance lies in showing how exploitation often requires cooperation, not because victims want harm, but because stability feels fragile.

Even the dialogue reflects this imbalance. Nina's compliments are double-edged. Praise is followed by correction. Kindness is paired with withdrawal. Andrew's assurances lack specificity, offering emotional cover without commitment. The language of the household is carefully calibrated to keep Millie off balance while believing she is being treated well.

Time itself feels distorted. The first day stretches. Moments repeat. The lack of clear markers creates a sense of suspension, echoing psychological states associated with stress and uncertainty. The outside world fades quickly. Phone calls are brief. Connections dissolve. The house becomes totalizing.

By the end of this opening movement, nothing overtly catastrophic has occurred. That is precisely the point. The film establishes that danger does not always announce itself. Sometimes it arrives as opportunity. Sometimes it wears generosity. Sometimes it asks nothing more than silence, gratitude, and the willingness to ignore what feels wrong because acknowledging it would mean losing everything you have just gained.

And in the years following the economic shocks of 2020, that bargain feels uncomfortably familiar.

Chapter Two

Millie Calloway — A Past That Never Stays Buried

"Nearly two-thirds of people released from prison in the United States between 2010 and 2020 reported hiding their criminal history when applying for work, not out of deceit, but fear." That statistic, echoed across reentry studies published in the decade following the Great Recession, frames the psychological terrain in which Millie Calloway exists when *The Housemaid (2025)* opens. Long before the first overt act of cruelty or manipulation appears on screen, Millie's inner life is already shaped by a decade-long national reality: in the United States between 2010 and 2024, a criminal record did not expire socially, even when it did legally. Reinvention was possible only if it was silent, incomplete, and constantly defended.

Millie arrives at the Winchester home not merely seeking employment but attempting a controlled erasure. Her posture, speech, and restraint reveal a woman performing acceptability in real time. She is cautious with eye contact, careful with phrasing, and deferential beyond necessity. These are not personality quirks; they are survival habits developed in response to what sociologists throughout the 2010s described as "anticipatory stigma," the expectation of rejection before it occurs. Millie has learned, as many formerly incarcerated individuals did during this period, that disclosure invites judgment and silence invites survival. The film captures this not through exposition but through behavior: how she answers questions without elaboration, how she absorbs discomfort without protest, how she accepts conditions she would otherwise refuse.

Between 2010 and 2024, reentry research consistently documented the emotional labor required of people attempting to "start over." Studies from the National Institute of Justice and the Prison Policy Initiative showed that individuals with records often self-monitor to an exhausting degree, editing their language, facial expressions, and emotional responses to avoid confirming negative stereotypes. Millie embodies this phenomenon early in the film. She does not react when she is subtly insulted. She does not correct assumptions. She anticipates blame before it is assigned. The audience watches her make these choices without hearing her internal monologue, which is precisely the point. The silence mirrors the real experience of reentry, where explanation rarely helps and self-containment becomes a shield.

Reinvention, in this context, is not aspirational. It is defensive. Millie's desire to begin again is inseparable from the fear of being found out, a fear intensified by the domestic setting. Unlike a workplace where boundaries are formal and time-limited, the Winchester home demands constant presence. There is no clocking out from scrutiny. Every interaction becomes evaluative. This aligns with findings from reintegration studies published between 2012 and 2019, which noted that formerly incarcerated individuals often avoid live-in or socially immersive jobs because exposure increases the risk of discovery. Millie accepts that risk anyway, which signals not optimism but desperation. She does not believe better options exist.

The film's early scenes show how shame operates as a regulating force. Millie cleans not just thoroughly but obsessively. She apologizes preemptively. She interprets neutral behavior as potential displeasure. Shame here is not loud or theatrical; it is quiet and procedural. Criminologists writing in the early 2000s described this as internalized control, where individuals police themselves more harshly than any authority figure would. By the 2010s, this concept had expanded to include "learned submission," a pattern observed among people who had spent extended time under institutional discipline. Millie's willingness to accept discomfort is not a flaw of character but the residue of that conditioning.

The emotional cost of hiding one's past is cumulative. Each omission requires vigilance. Each interaction becomes a calculation. The film subtly marks this through Millie's exhaustion. She is not physically overworked in the opening act, yet she appears drained. Her fatigue is psychological, the result of continuous self-censorship. Reentry research between 2015 and 2022 repeatedly emphasized that secrecy, while protective in the short term, erodes self-trust over time. When a person must constantly edit themselves to be accepted, they begin to doubt their right to occupy space at all. Millie's hesitation to assert even basic needs reflects this erosion.

Her criminal history, though initially undefined in detail, functions as an invisible weight shaping every decision. She does not evaluate the Winchesters' behavior according to fairness; she evaluates it according to tolerability. This distinction matters. Studies on post-incarceration psychology published between 2008 and 2020 found that individuals with records often recalibrate their expectations downward, accepting conditions others would reject because they believe discomfort is the price of inclusion. Millie's tolerance for mistreatment is not ignorance; it is negotiation. She is constantly measuring how much she can endure without jeopardizing her fragile foothold.

The Winchester household responds to this vulnerability in ways that are subtle enough to feel plausible. Exploitation does not arrive as overt cruelty at first. It appears as inconsistency, as shifting expectations, as emotional unpredictability that keeps Millie off balance. Whether this behavior is unconscious or deliberate becomes less important than its effect. Psychological literature from the early 2000s onward has shown that power imbalances often function most efficiently when the dominant party does not need to articulate them. The Winchesters sense, intuitively or otherwise, that Millie will not push back. Her record has already done that work for them.

What makes this dynamic particularly unsettling is how familiar it feels. Between 2010 and 2024, public discourse increasingly acknowledged systemic barriers faced by formerly incarcerated individuals, yet those acknowledgments rarely translated into daily interactions. Employers, landlords, and social institutions continued to treat criminal history as a moral failing rather than a completed sentence. The film places the audience in this contradiction. Viewers are invited to sympathize with Millie, yet they are also conditioned to scrutinize her. Her secrecy becomes suspicious. Her compliance becomes concerning. The same instincts society applies to people with records are mirrored in the viewing experience.

This conditioning is deliberate. Early in the

film, Millie's restraint can be misread as passivity or dishonesty. The audience, like the Winchesters, is left to fill in the gaps. This reflects a broader cultural pattern identified in media studies between 2010 and 2018, where narratives involving formerly incarcerated characters often position them as unreliable until proven otherwise. The burden of proof rests entirely on them. Millie must earn trust she has not been allowed to define on her own terms.

Shame, in this framework, becomes a tool others can leverage. When a person already believes they deserve less, they require less persuasion to accept it. Reintegration studies from 2000 to 2022 consistently warned that internalized guilt makes individuals more susceptible to coercion, particularly in environments where authority is ambiguous rather than explicit. The Winchester home exemplifies this ambiguity. There are no clear rules, only moods. No explicit threats, only implications. Millie's past teaches her that questioning authority invites punishment, so she adapts by absorbing discomfort silently.

Her self-monitoring extends beyond behavior into emotion. She regulates not just what she says, but what she allows herself to feel. Anger is suppressed. Suspicion is reframed as gratitude. Fear is interpreted as personal weakness rather than environmental danger. Psychologists studying post-institutional adjustment between 2005 and 2015 noted that many individuals learn to distrust their instincts after prolonged periods of punishment for independent thought. Millie's early choices reflect this learned distrust. When something feels wrong, she assumes she is misinterpreting it.

The film's portrayal of "starting over" avoids romanticism. There is no clean slate, only a fragile performance that must be maintained. Millie's past is not simply something that happened; it is something that continues to act upon her. Every decision she makes is filtered through the question of what she can afford to risk. Can she speak up? Can she leave? Can she be honest? The answer, shaped by years of social exclusion, is almost always no.

Between 2010 and 2024, policy discussions around second chances often emphasized employment statistics and recidivism rates, but the psychological dimension received less attention. *The Housemaid* fills that gap by showing how the fear of being seen as disposable alters a person's internal calculus. Millie does not stay because she is naïve. She stays because she understands, with painful clarity, how quickly opportunities disappear for people like her.

The audience's role in this dynamic is uncomfortable by design. Viewers are encouraged to ask themselves when their sympathy becomes conditional. At what point does Millie's secrecy feel like deception? At what point does her silence feel complicit? These questions mirror those faced by millions of Americans with records during the same period. Trust, the film suggests, is not withheld because of present behavior but because of past labels that refuse to fade.

Millie Calloway's early journey in *The Housemaid (2025)* is not defined by a single bad choice or moral failing. It is defined by adaptation to a society that promised redemption while quietly rationing it. Her reinvention is meticulous because it has to be. Her desperation is rational because alternatives are scarce. The price of survival, as the film makes clear, is not paid all at once. It is paid in silence, in compliance, in the slow erosion of one's sense of entitlement to safety and dignity.

Chapter Three

Nina Winchester — Charm, Volatility, and Control

"Gaslighting is not a single lie. It is a system of lies delivered so consistently that the victim begins to distrust their own perception of reality." — adapted from clinical psychology literature, mid-20th century

By the time Nina Winchester is first introduced in *The Housemaid (2025)*, nothing about her appears overtly threatening. Her smile is practiced but warm. Her voice carries the calm authority of someone accustomed to being obeyed without having to raise it. She welcomes Millie into the Winchester home with a polished ease that suggests generosity, refinement, and emotional openness. This initial charm is not accidental. It is deliberate, controlled, and rehearsed. Nina's hospitality operates as a performance, one that sets expectations not only for Millie, but for the audience itself. In psychological terms, this aligns with what clinical researchers between the mid-1990s and early 2000s identified as surface prosocial behavior masking deeper patterns of emotional dominance—behavior often associated with certain instability and control-oriented personality structures.

Early scenes present Nina as the ideal employer. She compliments Millie's work, offers reassurance, and frames herself as someone who values honesty and trust. Yet even within these moments of warmth, there are fissures.

Her praise arrives abruptly and disappears just as quickly. Her kindness is often paired with an undercurrent of scrutiny, a prolonged gaze, or a subtle correction that feels unnecessary. Studies published between 1995 and 2015 on emotional volatility, particularly those examining dominance-driven interpersonal behavior, describe this exact pattern: warmth used strategically, followed by withdrawal or criticism, creating an emotional imbalance that leaves the recipient striving to regain approval.

The first notable shift occurs not through overt cruelty, but through contradiction. Nina offers Millie clear instructions one day, only to chastise her the next for following them too precisely. In one scene, Nina thanks Millie for keeping the house spotless, commenting on her attention to detail, only to later accuse her of being obsessive and invasive. The tonal shift is jarring. This is emotional whiplash by design. Psychological literature from the early 2000s identifies unpredictability as a key mechanism of dominance. When rules change without warning, control is no longer enforced through authority but through confusion. The victim begins to monitor themselves obsessively, attempting to anticipate the next shift.

What makes Nina's volatility particularly unsettling is its cyclical nature. She does not remain cruel. After moments of hostility, she returns to warmth, sometimes apologetic, sometimes affectionate, often framing her behavior as stress-induced or misunderstood. This aligns with emotional instability frameworks explored in studies between 1998 and 2012, which note that oscillation between affection and aggression can be more destabilizing than consistent hostility. Consistency allows adaptation; unpredictability erodes confidence. Nina's cycles are not random. They escalate gradually. Each time Millie adjusts her behavior to accommodate Nina's mood, the threshold for acceptable conduct shifts again.

By mid-film, Nina's volatility begins to dominate the emotional climate of the house. Her anger no longer requires provocation. A misplaced object, a misunderstood tone, or even silence becomes justification. Yet she rarely raises her voice. Instead, she sharpens her words, delivering them with a controlled

52

intensity that implies reasonableness. This method mirrors dominance strategies discussed in psychological dominance research from the late 1990s, where authority is asserted not through volume, but through the implication that the subordinate is irrational or incompetent.

Nina's unpredictability becomes her most effective tool. Millie is left constantly reassessing her own behavior, replaying conversations, questioning whether she misheard or misunderstood. This is where Nina's charm and volatility converge into something more dangerous: gaslighting. The term itself originates from the 1944 film *Gaslight*, but its clinical definition was formalized through psychological research in the decades that followed, particularly gaining traction in diagnostic and abuse literature during the 2000s and 2010s. Gaslighting is not merely lying. It is the systematic undermining of another person's perception of reality through denial, contradiction, and manipulation.

Nina employs classic gaslighting tactics with precision. When confronted about her earlier instructions, she denies giving them. When Millie recalls a conversation accurately, Nina reframes it, insisting that Millie misunderstood her tone or intention. In one sequence, Nina accuses Millie of overstepping boundaries, only to later claim she encouraged initiative from the beginning. The contradiction is never acknowledged. Instead, Nina positions herself as consistent and Millie as confused. Research from the early 2010s emphasizes that gaslighting often succeeds not because the manipulator is convincing, but because the victim lacks external validation. Millie, isolated within the Winchester home and burdened by her own past, has no stable reference point to confirm her reality.

The film reinforces this psychological erosion through repetition. Each gaslighting incident on its own might seem minor. Together, they form a pattern that exhausts Millie emotionally. Confusion becomes constant. Self-doubt replaces certainty. Clinical studies between 2005 and 2015 on emotional abuse note that cognitive fatigue is a key outcome of prolonged gaslighting. Victims become less likely to challenge false narratives, not because they believe them, but because resistance feels futile.

Nina's gaslighting also extends beyond direct interaction. She manipulates the environment itself. Objects are moved and then blamed on Millie. Conversations are selectively remembered. Events are reframed in ways that cast Nina as the wronged party. When Millie reacts emotionally, Nina uses that reaction as evidence of instability. This tactic is well-documented in psychological abuse literature from the late 1990s onward, where emotional responses to mistreatment are weaponized to discredit the victim.

One of the most destabilizing aspects of Nina's behavior is her ability to appear credible. Wealth, social standing, and composure lend her authority. Studies on credibility bias published between 2000 and 2010 consistently demonstrate that individuals perceived as successful or composed are more likely to be believed, even in the face of contradictory evidence. Nina understands this intuitively. She never appears frantic in front of others. Her volatility is largely private. In public-facing moments, she is gracious, articulate, and controlled. This duality deepens Millie's isolation. When everyone else sees kindness, Millie begins to question her own experience.

As Nina's gaslighting intensifies, she introduces contradiction at a faster pace. One day, Millie is praised as indispensable. The next, she is threatened with dismissal. The oscillation accelerates. According to dominance research published between 2008 and 2015, increasing the frequency of emotional shifts heightens dependency. The victim becomes preoccupied with stabilizing the relationship, even at the expense of their own well-being. Nina does not need to explicitly demand loyalty. Millie's fear of losing stability ensures compliance.

The audience experiences this destabilization alongside Millie. The film deliberately withholds objective confirmation. Scenes are framed to emphasize ambiguity. Dialogue overlaps. Recollections conflict. This mirrors the experiential reality of gaslighting victims described in psychological literature throughout the 2010s, where the line between memory and manipulation blurs. The viewer is placed inside the confusion, forced to grapple with the same uncertainty that defines Millie's daily existence.

What makes Nina's behavior particularly

effective is that it is never framed as overt villainy. She presents herself as reasonable, even wounded. When challenged, she reframes her actions as reactions. Stress becomes her justification. Sensitivity becomes her defense. This aligns with studies from the late 1990s on moral disengagement, where individuals rationalize harmful behavior by framing themselves as victims of circumstance. Nina's volatility is always contextualized, never owned.

Over time, unpredictability ceases to appear as instability and instead functions as authority. Millie learns that stability depends not on fairness, but on Nina's mood. This inversion of power is central to Nina's control. Emotional chaos keeps Millie reactive rather than reflective. Each moment is about survival, not analysis. Psychological research from 2012 onward highlights this survival focus as a key outcome of prolonged emotional abuse. Higher cognitive processing gives way to immediate threat management.

Nina's charm, when it resurfaces, becomes even more potent. After cruelty, kindness feels like relief. This intermittent reinforcement mirrors behavioral conditioning principles studied extensively throughout the 20th century and applied to abuse dynamics in research from the 2000s. Unpredictable rewards create stronger attachments than consistent ones. Millie does not cling to Nina despite the abuse; she clings because of it.

By the latter portion of the film, Nina's

gaslighting has achieved its goal. Millie no longer trusts her instincts. She hesitates before speaking. She second-guesses her memories. The audience, too, is left questioning motivations and truth. Nina has not simply dominated the household; she has reshaped reality within it. Emotional exhaustion replaces resistance. Control no longer needs enforcement. It has been internalized.

What emerges from Nina Winchester is not a portrait of chaos, but of calculated disorder. Her volatility is not a flaw; it is a strategy refined through repetition and reinforced by power. Psychological frameworks between 1995 and 2015 repeatedly emphasize that dominance does not require consistency—only credibility and control over perception. Nina possesses both.

In *The Housemaid (2025)*, Nina's smiling hospitality is not a contradiction to her cruelty; it is its foundation. Her charm lowers defenses. Her volatility destabilizes boundaries. Her gaslighting fractures reality. Together, they form a closed system where control is maintained not through force, but through confusion, fear, and dependency. Long before the film reaches its overt twists, Nina has already won the most important battle: she has made truth negotiable.

Chapter Four

The Winchester House as a Psychological Trap

"Architecture is not neutral. It shapes behavior long before a word is spoken."

— Environmental psychology lecture notes, University of California, late 1980s

By the early 1990s, filmmakers had already learned that walls could intimidate more effectively than weapons. Domestic thrillers of that era began to treat houses not as backgrounds but as systems—structures that guide movement, restrict vision, and quietly enforce obedience. From *Sleeping with the Enemy* (1991) to *The Hand That Rocks the Cradle* (1992), space itself became an instrument of pressure. By the time *The Housemaid (2025)* arrives, that lesson has been refined to something colder and more surgical. The Winchester house does not threaten Millie with violence. It does something far more efficient: it teaches her where she belongs.

The first thing the house establishes is scale. Large enough to suggest wealth, but not grand enough to feel public, it sits in the uneasy middle ground between luxury and enclosure. This design choice matters. Mansions in earlier thrillers often overwhelmed characters with size alone, but post-2000 domestic thrillers increasingly favored homes that feel intimate yet controlling. The Winchester house reflects that shift. Its corridors are not endless; they are precise. Its rooms are not sprawling; they are arranged with intent. Every doorway seems to lead somewhere meaningful, and that meaning is never neutral.

Between 1990 and 2025, domestic architecture in thrillers evolved alongside cultural anxieties about privacy, surveillance, and power. In the early 1990s, control was visual and overt—mirrors, open staircases, long sightlines that allowed one character to watch another from a distance. By the 2010s, influenced by the rise of smart homes and digital monitoring, control became quieter. Doors closed softly. Cameras were implied rather than shown. The Winchester house belongs to this later lineage. It rarely announces its authority. It simply assumes it.

Locked doors are the most obvious expression

of that authority, but their real function is psychological rather than physical. Environmental psychology research from the 1970s onward—particularly the work of Irwin Altman and later Edward Hall—demonstrated that perceived control over space matters more than actual restriction. A door does not need to be locked constantly to create anxiety; it only needs to be locked once, unexpectedly. In the Winchester house, certain rooms are closed without explanation. Others are accessible but socially forbidden. The distinction matters. Millie is not restrained. She is conditioned.

Sightlines do much of the work. From kitchens that open into living areas to staircases positioned so movement is always visible, the house ensures that Millie is rarely unseen, yet never fully observed. This ambiguity mirrors surveillance models studied in the late twentieth century, particularly Michel Foucault's discussion of the panopticon, which reentered popular academic discourse in the 1990s. The power of surveillance, Foucault argued, lies in uncertainty. The Winchester house embodies that principle. Millie does not know when she is being watched, only that she might be. That possibility is enough.

Isolation is enforced through design choices that appear polite on the surface. The house is set apart from neighbors, not dramatically, but sufficiently to discourage casual contact. Windows frame landscapes rather than streets. Outdoor spaces are expansive but exposed, offering visibility without connection. Studies published between 1985 and 2005 on spatial isolation showed that environments limiting incidental social interaction increased feelings of vulnerability, even when physical comfort was high. The Winchester house offers comfort generously—clean lines, soft lighting, controlled temperature—while quietly removing unpredictability. Comfort becomes a substitute for freedom.

Bedrooms reveal the hierarchy more clearly than any spoken rule. Millie's room is not hidden in a basement, as earlier thrillers might have chosen. Instead, it is placed just far enough from the family's private spaces to reinforce separation without cruelty. Environmental psychology research from the 1970s through the early 2000s consistently found that room placement communicates status more effectively than size. Proximity to shared areas signals belonging; distance signals utility. Millie's room is functional, clean, and emotionally blank. It does not invite personalization. It tolerates her presence.

The Winchester bedrooms, by contrast, are both private and protected. Doors close completely. Sound does not travel easily. The difference is subtle but cumulative. Millie moves through spaces where her presence is assumed to be temporary, while the family occupies rooms designed for permanence. This division echoes sociological studies on domestic labor published between 1990 and 2015, which documented how live-in workers often internalized spatial boundaries as moral boundaries. Certain rooms became psychologically off-limits even when physically accessible. The Winchester house relies on that instinct.

Forbidden spaces do not announce themselves with signs or warnings. They are defined by tone. A pause before answering a question. A change in posture when Millie approaches a hallway. The house amplifies these cues. Narrow passages slow her pace. Corners block her view. The result is not fear in the conventional sense but caution—a constant low-level assessment of where she should and should not exist. Fear without threat is one of the most effective forms of control, a finding supported by behavioral studies from the 1980s that showed sustained anxiety was more debilitating than acute terror.

What makes the house particularly effective as a psychological trap is its consistency. It never contradicts itself. Doors remain doors. Rooms retain their function. There are no sudden spatial surprises. This stability reinforces the illusion that the house is reasonable, even as it limits Millie's autonomy. Research from the late 1990s on learned compliance demonstrated that individuals were more likely to accept restrictions in environments that appeared orderly and predictable. Chaos invites resistance. Order invites adaptation.

Between 2000 and 2020, domestic thrillers increasingly explored this idea, shifting away from violent confrontations toward environments that erode agency slowly. Films like *The Others* (2001), *The Gift* (2015), and *Parasite* (2019) used architecture to encode class, threat, and belonging. *The Housemaid (2025)* extends this tradition but localizes it within a single character's daily routine. The house does not need dramatic reveals. Its power lies in repetition. Each day reinforces the same spatial lesson: move here, not there; stop now; wait.

Sound design reinforces architectural control. Floors that creak selectively. Doors that close too softly to announce themselves. These details align with acoustic environment studies conducted between 1975 and 2000, which found that unpredictable sound patterns increased stress responses even in familiar spaces. Millie is never startled by noise. She is unsettled by its absence. Silence becomes another boundary.

The idea that spaces can "watch back" is not metaphorical in this context. Mirrors are placed where reflection is unavoidable, not for vanity but for awareness. Glass surfaces create layered visibility, allowing characters to be seen without direct eye contact. This design choice mirrors findings from environmental psychology in the 1980s that suggested reflective surfaces heightened self-monitoring behavior. Millie becomes aware of herself as an object within the space. She adjusts posture, tone, even facial expression, as if the house itself were evaluating her.

What distinguishes the Winchester house from earlier cinematic homes is its restraint. It does not scream wealth. It whispers entitlement. By the 2020s, cultural conversations around power had shifted from overt domination to subtle systems. The house reflects that shift. It does not need locks on every door, cameras in every corner, or guards at the gate. It relies on social expectations reinforced by architecture. Millie's compliance feels voluntary because the environment never explicitly demands it.

The absence of overt threats is essential. Environmental psychology studies from 1970 to 2010 repeatedly emphasized that perceived lack of choice, rather than force, produced the strongest feelings of entrapment. Millie is free to leave in theory. In practice, the house has already taught her what leaving would mean: exposure, instability, loss of the fragile order she depends on. The architecture does not trap her body. It traps her calculations.

Time behaves differently inside the house. Rooms are lit to obscure natural rhythms. Windows frame views that do not change significantly throughout the day. Research from the late 1980s on circadian disruption in controlled environments showed that altered light exposure increased dependency and reduced initiative. The Winchester house does not eliminate time; it smooths it. Days blur. Urgency fades. Decisions feel less immediate. This temporal flattening supports the broader system of control.

Between 1990 and 2025, as domestic thrillers increasingly centered women navigating private danger, houses became arenas where power operated invisibly. *The Housemaid* situates itself firmly within that evolution. The Winchester house is not haunted. It is optimized. Every design choice, from room placement to sound absorption, contributes to a single outcome: Millie's gradual internalization of her place.

The most unsettling aspect is how reasonable it all appears. Nothing in the house is overtly cruel. There are no chains, no barred windows, no locked basements. Yet by the time Millie understands the rules, they feel natural. This mirrors findings from social psychology experiments conducted between the 1960s and 1990s, including studies on institutional behavior, which showed that environments could normalize inequality without explicit enforcement.

The house does not need to speak. It does not need to threaten. It simply exists, shaping behavior through repetition and design. By the mid-2020s, this approach to cinematic space feels less like fiction and more like reflection. Modern homes increasingly integrate surveillance, automation, and controlled access. *The Housemaid (2025)* exaggerates none of this. It merely arranges familiar elements into a pattern that reveals how easily space can become strategy.

Millie's fear is never loud. It accumulates. It is the hesitation before opening a door. The awareness of footsteps behind her. The instinct to stay in her room even when nothing explicitly prevents her from leaving it.

Environmental psychologists in the early 2000s described this phenomenon as "anticipatory compliance"—behavior shaped not by rules, but by expectation. The Winchester house excels at creating expectation.

In this way, the house becomes the most reliable enforcer of hierarchy in the film. People fluctuate. Moods shift. Intentions blur. The architecture remains steady. It does not need motivation. It already knows its role.

Chapter Five

Andrew Winchester — Savior, Bystander, or Architect

"Power does not always announce itself with raised voices or clenched fists. Sometimes it arrives softly, in the form of patience, courtesy, and a man who never seems angry."

In *The Housemaid (2025)*, Andrew Winchester exists in the spaces between action and inaction, between concern and control. He is not loud, not volatile, not overtly cruel. He does not slam doors or erupt the way Nina does. Instead, he listens. He pauses. He offers reassurance in measured tones. This restraint is precisely what makes him dangerous. In psychological thrillers of the early 2000s, antagonism often arrived with visible menace. By the 2010s and into the mid-2020s, cinema increasingly shifted toward quieter figures of authority—men whose power lies not in what they do, but in what they allow to happen. Andrew Winchester belongs squarely in that lineage.

From his earliest appearance, Andrew is framed as reasonable. He speaks gently. He rarely interrupts. He asks questions rather than issuing commands. This presentation draws from a modern masculine ideal that gained cultural prominence between roughly 2005 and 2020: the controlled, emotionally literate man who does not need to dominate overtly to remain in charge. In film and television, this archetype replaced earlier models of explosive masculinity that dominated the 1980s and

1990s. Andrew's authority is understated, but it is never absent. The household moves according to rhythms he does not need to enforce. His silence functions as permission.

Masculinity in cinema during the early 2000s often centered on crisis—men struggling with relevance, control, or emotional articulation. By the time audiences reached the post-2015 era, restraint itself had become a signifier of power. Andrew embodies this shift. He does not compete with Nina's volatility; he contains it. He does not challenge her behavior publicly; he absorbs it privately. In doing so, he creates a moral fog where responsibility becomes difficult to assign. The film repeatedly places him at moments where intervention would be simple, yet he chooses distance. This distance is framed as politeness, but politeness does not neutralize consequence.

The question the film quietly insists on asking is whether Andrew's restraint is a sign of ethical hesitation or calculated withdrawal. The difference matters. Ethical hesitation implies inner conflict, a man paralyzed by uncertainty. Strategic distance suggests awareness without accountability. Andrew's behavior consistently leans toward the latter. He sees enough to know something is wrong. He hears enough to understand Millie's fear. He chooses restraint anyway. In psychological terms, this aligns with what behavioral researchers between 1990 and 2010 identified as passive facilitation—when individuals enable harm not through direct action, but through refusal to disrupt a harmful system.

Andrew's politeness becomes a social shield. When he speaks kindly to Millie, it signals safety. When he refrains from raising his voice, it suggests reasonableness. These cues exploit deeply ingrained social heuristics. Studies on authority bias from the 1970s through the early 2000s demonstrated that people often equate calm demeanor with moral reliability. Andrew benefits from this cognitive shortcut. Millie does not see him as a threat because he does not look like one. The film understands this psychology and weaponizes it.

Between 2000 and 2025, representations of male antagonists evolved toward ambiguity. Films increasingly asked audiences to interrogate not just cruelty, but compliance.

Andrew is not framed as a villain in the traditional sense. He is framed as a man who could stop something and does not. That choice reflects broader cultural conversations that gained traction after 2010, particularly around institutional harm and bystander responsibility. Andrew is not outside the system of abuse within the Winchester home. He is central to its stability.

His authority is reinforced by class, gender, and social credibility. As a wealthy homeowner, his version of events would carry weight. As a calm man, his words would be trusted. Millie understands this intuitively, even before she articulates it. Her interactions with Andrew are shaped by an awareness that his approval could protect her, while his disapproval could erase her. This imbalance is never explicitly stated, but it governs every exchange. Andrew does not need to threaten Millie. His position does the work for him.

There are moments when Andrew appears protective. He intervenes subtly. He asks if Millie is all right. He offers explanations that soften Nina's behavior. These moments are crucial, not because they absolve him, but because they complicate him. Sympathy becomes his most effective tool. Research on trust formation conducted between the 1980s and early 2000s consistently found that intermittent kindness creates stronger emotional bonds than consistent support. Andrew's kindness is precisely that—intermittent. It arrives just often enough to keep Millie hopeful.

Hope, in this context, is dangerous. Millie's need for validation is rooted in her past, shaped by years of social rejection and moral judgment. Individuals with histories of institutional punishment often develop heightened sensitivity to approval cues, a phenomenon documented extensively in psychological studies between 1995 and 2018. Andrew's attention, however mild, carries disproportionate weight. When he listens, she feels seen. When he reassures, she feels believed. This emotional response clouds her assessment of risk.

Trust is not built through grand gestures in *The Housemaid*. It is built through proximity and tone. Andrew's voice is steady. His posture is open. These nonverbal signals align with trust markers identified in behavioral research as early as the 1980s. The film repeatedly places Andrew in situations where his physical presence calms tension. This calm is deceptive. It diffuses urgency. It encourages Millie to wait rather than act. Waiting benefits the system she is trapped inside.

Sympathy, when paired with power, becomes leverage. Andrew does not need to manipulate overtly. He simply allows Millie to believe he might help. That belief keeps her compliant longer than fear alone could. Betrayal studies from the 1990s onward emphasize that perceived allies who fail to act cause deeper psychological damage than obvious adversaries. Andrew occupies this exact position. When he does not intervene decisively, the absence feels personal.

His restraint also serves to isolate responsibility. Nina's volatility draws attention. She becomes the visible problem. Andrew fades into the background, where his inaction is harder to scrutinize. This dynamic mirrors real-world patterns observed in organizational abuse cases between 2000 and 2020, where charismatic or volatile figures attract blame while quieter enablers remain unexamined. The film does not allow Andrew this escape, even if the characters do.

Millie's judgment is compromised not because she is naive, but because she is emotionally depleted. The desire to be believed, to be protected by someone credible, overrides caution. Andrew's occasional affirmations reinforce the illusion that endurance will be rewarded. This illusion is central to many abusive systems. The promise of eventual relief becomes a mechanism of control. Andrew never explicitly makes that promise. He simply allows it to exist.

Andrew Winchester reflects a broader cinematic reckoning with masculinity that emerged strongly after 2015. Audiences were increasingly invited to question not just aggressive dominance, but benevolent authority. The man who claims neutrality while benefiting from harm is no longer invisible. Andrew is written and performed as a figure who understands the dynamics at play yet chooses comfort over confrontation. His moral ambiguity is not confusion; it is selection.

The danger of trusting Andrew lies in his

consistency. He is consistently calm. Consistently polite. Consistently noncommittal. This consistency creates predictability, and predictability feels safe. Trust research from the early 2000s demonstrates that predictability often outweighs moral clarity in relationship formation. Millie does not trust Andrew because he is good. She trusts him because he is stable.

By the time the audience begins to question Andrew's role, the damage is already done. His restraint has allowed the environment to calcify. His silence has validated cruelty. His sympathy has delayed resistance. The film resists simplifying him into a single category. He is not a savior. He is not merely a bystander. He is a participant whose power lies in what he withholds.

Andrew Winchester stands as one of the most unsettling figures in *The Housemaid (2025)* precisely because he feels familiar. He resembles men who pride themselves on reasonableness, who avoid conflict, who believe that not choosing sides is a moral position. The film situates him within a cultural moment increasingly aware that neutrality often favors the powerful. Andrew's story is not about evil intent. It is about the quiet preservation of control through restraint, and the cost of mistaking calm for conscience.

Chapter Six

Class, Wealth, and Invisible Power

"In 1910, domestic service was the single largest occupation for women in the United States. More than one in four working women cleaned, cooked, or cared for families who were not their own." That statistic, drawn from early U.S. labor records, is not a historical footnote—it is the foundation on which *The Housemaid (2025)* quietly stands. The film's tension does not begin with violence or deceit. It begins with class. With who serves, who commands, and who is expected to endure in silence.

Domestic labor has always existed in the shadow of wealth. From the early 1900s, when servants lived in employers' homes under rigid moral and behavioral control, to the post–World War II era, when "help" became feminized and racialized, the role has been defined by intimacy without equality. The worker is close enough to see everything, yet distant enough to be dismissed. Millie Calloway enters the Winchester household in 2025 carrying the full weight of that history, even if she never names it. Her job title may be modern, her employer wealthy and polished, but the structure is unchanged: she eats after them, sleeps below them, and exists at their convenience.

Between 1900 and 1930, domestic workers in Western societies were often young women with limited education, many of them migrants or members of marginalized racial groups. They lived where they worked, were monitored constantly, and could be dismissed without explanation. By the 1950s and 1960s, as labor laws expanded and middle-class households shifted, domestic work did not disappear—it became less visible. Caregivers, cleaners, nannies, and live-in aides remained largely unprotected by the same labor standards applied elsewhere. This invisibility is crucial to understanding Millie's vulnerability. She is not simply underpaid or overworked. She is structurally unprotected.

Millie's economic position in *The Housemaid* reflects a reality well documented between 2000 and 2020. Studies from the International Labour Organization consistently showed that domestic workers were among the least regulated labor groups worldwide, with high rates of wage theft, emotional abuse, and dismissal without recourse. In the United States, live-in domestic workers were excluded from many federal labor protections until incremental reforms in the 2010s. Even then, enforcement remained weak. When Millie accepts the job despite its odd conditions, she is behaving rationally within an unequal system. Economic desperation does not sharpen caution; it dulls it.

Wealth operates in the film not as excess, but as insulation. The Winchester family's money does not merely buy comfort—it buys credibility. Sociological research from the 1990s onward repeatedly demonstrated that affluent individuals are more likely to be perceived as trustworthy, stable, and rational, even when engaging in erratic or harmful behavior. Nina Winchester's volatility is read as eccentricity. Andrew's silence is read as dignity. Millie's discomfort, by contrast, is read as instability. This imbalance is not accidental. It mirrors real-world patterns documented in family court cases, employment disputes, and domestic abuse reports between 1990 and 2020, where the word of an employer routinely outweighed that of a dependent worker.

Domestic workers occupy a strange psychological space. They are expected to be invisible yet emotionally available, obedient yet intuitive, loyal yet disposable. Millie's role demands that she notice everything while pretending not to. She sees what the family eats, how they speak to one another, which rooms are locked, which moods dominate the day. Historically, this has always been the servant's position: a witness without standing. In Edwardian households, servants knew about affairs, debts, and violence long before outsiders did. Their knowledge rarely protected them. In *The Housemaid*, this inherited imbalance is modernized but unchanged.

Caregiving work, particularly when performed by women, has long been associated with moral obligation rather than professional boundaries. Between 1970 and 2010, feminist labor scholars repeatedly argued that care work was undervalued precisely because it was seen as an extension of "natural" female behavior. Millie's labor is framed not as skilled or contractual, but as something she should be grateful to perform.

Gratitude becomes currency. Gratitude replaces safety. When Nina treats her poorly, the unspoken rule is that Millie should absorb it because she has been given an opportunity.

The film's quiet cruelty lies in how normal this dynamic feels. Nothing about Millie's treatment initially appears illegal. It appears personal, emotional, subjective. That ambiguity is the shield wealth relies on. Abusive power does not need to shout when it can reframe. Nina's behavior is not presented as abuse by those around her; it is presented as stress, illness, or temperament. Andrew's inaction is not labeled complicity; it is framed as neutrality. Millie's reactions are scrutinized more closely than the actions that provoke them.

Between 1995 and 2015, research on workplace

credibility bias showed that employees with less social capital were more likely to self-censor complaints, anticipating dismissal or retaliation. Millie embodies this anticipation. Her silence is not passive. It is strategic. She understands, intuitively, that speaking will cost her more than enduring. This awareness shapes every choice she makes. When she questions herself, when she apologizes unnecessarily, when she minimizes her own fear, she is responding to a hierarchy she knows she cannot win against.

The question of who gets believed sits at the center of *The Housemaid*. Legal scholars have long documented that credibility is not distributed evenly. Studies of court proceedings between 1990 and 2010 showed that defendants and plaintiffs from lower socioeconomic backgrounds were more likely to be perceived as unreliable, emotional, or deceptive. These perceptions were often unconscious, reinforced by language, appearance, and demeanor. Millie anticipates this judgment. Her criminal past compounds it. She knows that if narratives collide, hers will lose.

This expectation shapes her silence long before any explicit threat appears. Silence becomes a form of self-preservation. It is also a trap. Sociological research from the early 2000s highlighted how marginalized workers often internalize blame for mistreatment, believing endurance is proof of worthiness. Millie's internal monologue reflects this conditioning. She questions whether she is overreacting, whether she deserves better, whether survival requires submission. The film does not romanticize this mindset. It exposes it.

Domestic thrillers often frame class conflict as backdrop rather than engine. *The Housemaid* does the opposite. Every psychological turn is fueled by inequality. The house is not just large; it is hierarchical. The rules are unspoken but absolute. Millie's access to space, comfort, and even dignity is conditional. The Winchesters' access to forgiveness and reinterpretation is not.

Between 2010 and 2020, high-profile cases involving domestic workers and caregivers—many involving abuse dismissed for years—revealed how power delays accountability. Employers with resources can hire attorneys, shape narratives, and wait out accusations. Workers without resources must choose between speaking and surviving. Millie's fear of disbelief is not paranoia. It is statistically justified.

What makes the film unsettling is not that wealth corrupts, but that it protects. Nina's behavior would be alarming in a different context. In this one, it is normalized. Andrew's detachment would be suspicious if he lacked status. Here, it reads as restraint. The audience, like Millie, is invited to doubt itself. That doubt is the most effective form of control.

From 1900 to 2025, domestic labor has changed in language but not in structure. Titles softened. Conditions improved unevenly. Power remained asymmetrical. Millie's position is contemporary, but her vulnerability is historical. She is part of a lineage of workers whose proximity to wealth exposes them to its worst impulses without granting them its protection.

The film's psychological tension depends on this imbalance. Without class disparity, the story collapses. Without economic vulnerability, Millie would leave. Without credibility bias, she would speak. Without wealth shielding behavior, the Winchesters would be forced to account for themselves. Instead, the system works exactly as designed.

Millie's silence is not weakness. It is learned behavior shaped by decades of social conditioning. Her calculations mirror those made by countless real-world workers who understand that truth alone does not carry weight. Power decides which truths survive.

By grounding its horror in social reality rather than spectacle, *The Housemaid (2025)* reveals something uncomfortable: that the most frightening systems are not hidden or illegal, but familiar, polished, and socially acceptable. The danger is not that Millie is unseen. It is that she is seen—and still not believed.

Chapter Seven

Enzo and the Illusion of Escape

"The stranger you trust most is often the one who feels most like you."

— social psychology observation frequently echoed in research on perceived safety and affiliation, late 20th century

Enzo enters *The Housemaid (2025)* quietly, almost deliberately understated, and that restraint is precisely what makes him dangerous—not through malice, but through illusion. He is introduced not as a threat but as a counterweight to the oppressive emotional gravity of the Winchester household. Where the main house feels watched, controlled, and performative, Enzo's presence suggests openness, informality, and the promise of an unguarded space. He works outside, on the edges of the property, removed from the internal hierarchies that suffocate Millie. That physical distance mirrors the psychological one: Enzo appears separate from the power structure, uninvested in the domestic games unfolding inside the walls. For Millie, that separation reads as safety.

From the moment their interactions begin, the film subtly codes Enzo as an outsider in parallel to Millie. He is not family, not wealthy, not central. He occupies a liminal role—useful but peripheral, visible but overlooked. This shared marginalization forms the emotional basis of trust between them, a dynamic well documented in social psychology research between the

1970s and early 2000s. Henri Tajfel's work on social identity theory in the 1970s demonstrated how individuals form bonds not merely through similarity, but through shared exclusion. Being "not them" becomes more powerful than being alike in any concrete way. Enzo and Millie are bound less by who they are than by who they are not: not Winchesters, not protected, not believed.

That bond deepens through small moments rather than declarations. Casual conversations. Unmonitored exchanges. A tone that lacks the sharp edges Millie has learned to anticipate inside the house. Enzo does not interrogate her past. He does not demand explanations. He does not fluctuate between affection and cruelty. In psychological terms, he provides what researchers in the 1980s and 1990s described as a "low-threat affiliative environment," a space where vigilance can momentarily relax. For someone like Millie, whose survival has depended on constant self-monitoring since her incarceration and release, that relaxation feels like oxygen.

The danger lies in how quickly perceived safety becomes assumed safety. Studies on in-group bias throughout the late 20th century repeatedly showed that individuals are more likely to underestimate risk posed by those they categorize as part of their in-group—even when objective warning signs exist. Enzo's outsider status automatically places him on Millie's side in her internal narrative. He becomes "one of us," even though the definition of "us" is built on vulnerability rather than verified trust. The film exploits this cognitive shortcut with precision. It does not depict Enzo as overtly deceptive. Instead, it shows how little deception is required when hope does the work on its own.

Hope is one of the most dangerous emotions the film engages with, precisely because it masquerades as strength. Millie's hope is not abstract; it is situational and immediate. Hope that someone sees her as human rather than as labor. Hope that there is a witness to her experience. Hope that escape might be possible without confrontation, exposure, or sacrifice. Enzo becomes the vessel for that hope, not through promises, but through presence. Social psychology literature from the 1990s, particularly studies on perceived allyship, emphasizes that hope attached to another person often bypasses critical evaluation. The mind, under sustained stress, prioritizes relief over verification.

As their interactions continue, Enzo's role shifts from neutral companion to emotional refuge. This transition is subtle and crucial. Emotional refuge is not the same as safety; it is often sought precisely because safety feels unreachable. Refuge offers rest, not protection. The film underscores this distinction through timing and context. Millie turns to Enzo not when she is strongest, but when she is most depleted. Her boundaries are already eroded by gaslighting, isolation, and internalized self-doubt. In that state, even a fragile connection feels solid.

Desire enters the dynamic not as lust, but as validation. Desire tells Millie she is still wanted, still seen, still capable of inspiring care rather than suspicion. Research from the late 1970s onward consistently showed that desire, particularly when paired with affirmation, lowers risk perception. It narrows focus. It accelerates attachment. In the film, desire does not explode into melodrama; it unfolds through glances, shared confidences, and the gradual replacement of caution with intimacy. That intimacy is not reckless—it is earned emotionally, which makes it feel justified.

Yet intimacy, once introduced, demands secrecy. And secrecy, unlike privacy, always compounds vulnerability. The distinction is critical. Privacy protects autonomy; secrecy protects fear. Millie's connection with Enzo must remain hidden not because it is inherently wrong, but because exposure within the Winchester ecosystem carries consequences. Every concealed interaction increases the psychological load she carries. Studies on secrecy from the 1980s and 1990s demonstrated that secrets heighten emotional intensity while simultaneously reducing external reality checks. The fewer people who know, the fewer perspectives exist to challenge interpretation. Millie's world narrows further, even as she believes it is expanding.

The film carefully shows how secrecy rewires judgment. Actions that might otherwise trigger hesitation—meeting alone, sharing sensitive information, trusting plans without contingency—begin to feel necessary rather than risky. Desire accelerates this process. Desire reframes urgency as inevitability. In Millie's mind, delays become threats: if she waits, the opportunity disappears; if she hesitates, she loses the one space where she can breathe. This cognitive compression, documented in studies on stress and attachment throughout the 1990s and early 2000s, reduces long-term thinking in favor of immediate emotional payoff.

Enzo, importantly, does not orchestrate this shift with cruelty. His danger lies in passivity rather than intent. He is not a mastermind, nor is he a savior. He is human, limited, and constrained by his own position within the household's power structure. The film resists turning him into a villain because doing so would absolve the system that creates him. Enzo cannot truly protect Millie because protection requires leverage, visibility, and credibility—resources he does not possess. By framing him as an apparent ally without power, the narrative exposes a harsh truth: shared marginalization does not equal shared safety.

This realization arrives too late because hope has already taken root. Once hope exists, its loss becomes catastrophic. Research on hope theory from the late 20th century indicates that dashed hope produces sharper psychological collapse than sustained despair. Millie's belief in Enzo as an escape is not naïve; it is adaptive. It allows her to endure what would otherwise be unbearable. But adaptation in hostile environments often becomes maladaptive when circumstances shift. The very mechanism that keeps her going becomes the one that blinds her.

The cost of emotional refuge is revealed not in a single betrayal, but in accumulated miscalculations. Each private moment convinces Millie that she is no longer alone. Each shared secret convinces her that she has an ally. Each emotional exchange distances her further from objective assessment of risk. The film aligns the audience with her perspective so completely that viewers, too, want Enzo to be the answer. This alignment is intentional and unsettling. It forces recognition of how easily viewers themselves accept the illusion of escape when it feels emotionally earned.

By situating Enzo at the intersection of desire, secrecy, and hope, *The Housemaid* exposes a psychological trap that extends beyond the screen. The trap is not trusting the wrong person; it is trusting the right feelings in the wrong conditions. Enzo represents the fantasy that survival does not require confrontation—that relief can be found without cost. The film dismantles that fantasy slowly, showing that emotional refuge without structural safety is temporary by design.

As the consequences accelerate, it becomes clear that desire has not merely clouded Millie's threat assessment; it has reshaped it. Threat is no longer defined by danger, but by loss. The greatest fear becomes losing the refuge, not remaining in harm. This inversion, identified in trauma research throughout the early 2000s, explains why escape routes close even when they appear open. The mind protects the fragile source of hope at all costs, including self-preservation.

Enzo's role, then, is not to betray Millie, but to reveal the limits of solidarity under oppression. Shared marginalization can create connection, empathy, even love—but it cannot replace power, protection, or accountability. By the time this truth becomes unavoidable, the cost has already been paid in secrecy, misjudgment, and accelerated consequence. The illusion of escape dissolves, leaving behind a harsher understanding: in environments designed to isolate, hope is never neutral. It can sustain, but it can also expose. And once it takes shape in another person, letting go becomes far more dangerous than never believing at all.

Chapter Eight

Gaslighting as a Weapon

"Gaslighting is not about making someone crazy," wrote psychoanalyst Robin Stern in 2007. "It is about gaining control by making someone doubt their own reality." Long before the term became common language, its effects were already measurable. A 2018 study in the *Journal of Emotional Abuse* found that victims of psychological manipulation were more likely to question their own memory than to question their abuser, even when presented with contradictory evidence. This is the quiet terror at the center of *The Housemaid (2025)*—a terror that does not announce itself with violence, but with correction, contradiction, and the steady

erosion of certainty.

The word "gaslighting" enters the psychological lexicon through a work of fiction. In 1938, British playwright Patrick Hamilton wrote *Gas Light*, a stage play in which a husband manipulates his wife into believing she is mentally unstable by dimming the gas lights in their home and denying any change when she notices it. The story reached a wider audience with the 1944 Hollywood adaptation starring Ingrid Bergman, whose performance gave visual form to a manipulation strategy that would later be recognized clinically. By the late twentieth century, psychologists had begun to use "gaslighting" as a descriptor for a specific pattern of emotional abuse, one that relied not on threats or force, but on persistent denial, contradiction, and misdirection.

By the early 2000s, gaslighting appeared regularly in domestic abuse research, particularly in studies examining non-physical coercive control. In 2007, Stern defined gaslighting as a form of manipulation in which one person systematically undermines another's perception of reality, memory, and judgment, causing them to become dependent on the manipulator for truth. In 2019, the American Psychological Association formally described gaslighting as a tactic of emotional abuse that "seeks to sow doubt in a targeted individual, making them question their own memory, perception, or sanity." This definition matters when watching *The Housemaid*, because the film does not dramatize gaslighting as an abstract idea. It shows it unfolding minute by minute, correction by correction, until doubt becomes the dominant emotional state.

Millie Calloway enters the Winchester home already primed for self-doubt. Her criminal past, referenced through dialogue and guarded body language, situates her within a well-documented psychological vulnerability. Studies published between 2000 and 2015 on post-incarceration reintegration consistently show that individuals with criminal records are more likely to accept unfair treatment, believing it to be deserved. A 2013 report by the Urban Institute noted that formerly incarcerated individuals often internalize blame to such a degree that they interpret mistreatment as confirmation of their own moral failure rather than as abuse. This internalized shame becomes fertile ground for gaslighting.

From the earliest interactions, Nina Winchester corrects Millie in ways that seem trivial. A remark about where an object was placed. A disagreement about what was said the previous day. A tone that implies concern while delivering dismissal. In isolation, each moment feels inconsequential. Taken together, they form a pattern that mirrors clinical descriptions of gaslighting from the 2000s onward: the steady replacement of the victim's internal compass with the abuser's version of events.

One of the most effective tools of gaslighting is temporal confusion—challenging the victim's memory of when something occurred. In a 2009 study published in *Psychology of Women*

Quarterly, researchers found that repeated contradictions about timing led subjects to distrust their own recollection even when they were initially confident. In *The Housemaid*, this tactic appears in scenes where Nina insists Millie has been told rules she clearly has not, or denies giving instructions Millie remembers vividly. The camera lingers on Millie's hesitation, not because she is uncertain, but because she has been trained to hesitate. Her pause becomes the abuse made visible.

Gaslighting rarely begins with overt denial. Instead, it starts with concern. "Are you sure?" "You seem stressed." "You might be remembering it wrong." Clinical literature from the 2010s identifies this stage as "benevolent invalidation," a phase in which the manipulator frames doubt as care. Nina's dialogue frequently adopts this register. Her voice softens as she questions Millie's perception, creating a contradiction between tone and content that disarms resistance. The result is not immediate submission, but delayed confidence. Millie begins rehearsing conversations in her head, preemptively preparing for correction.

Andrew Winchester's role complicates the psychological terrain. Research on triangulation in abusive dynamics, particularly studies published between 2005 and 2020, shows that the presence of a seemingly neutral third party can intensify gaslighting by diffusing responsibility. When Andrew offers reassurance without intervention, he inadvertently validates Nina's version of events. His calm demeanor functions as corroboration, even when he says very little. In a 2014 analysis of coercive control published in *Violence Against Women*, scholars noted that silence from authority figures often reinforces the abuser's narrative more effectively than overt agreement.

Gaslighting does not rely on lies alone. It depends on repetition. Cognitive psychology research from the 1960s onward has demonstrated that familiarity increases perceived truth, a phenomenon known as the illusory truth effect. When Nina repeats her version of events calmly and consistently, it begins to feel more stable than Millie's lived experience, which is increasingly fraught with anxiety. The film visualizes this process through lighting and pacing. Conversations slow.

Corrections lengthen. Millie's reactions shrink.

By the mid-2010s, domestic abuse frameworks began emphasizing coercive control over isolated incidents. In 2015, the United Kingdom criminalized coercive control, recognizing patterns of psychological domination as abuse even in the absence of physical harm. Studies following this legislative shift found that victims of non-physical abuse reported higher levels of confusion, self-blame, and difficulty articulating their experiences than victims of physical violence. *The Housemaid* reflects this reality with unsettling accuracy. Millie cannot point to a single moment of undeniable wrongdoing. Instead, she exists within a fog of contradictions.

This fog is reinforced through isolation.

Domestic abuse research between 2000 and 2023 consistently identifies isolation as a core strategy of psychological abuse. A 2018 meta-analysis in *Trauma, Violence, & Abuse* concluded that emotional abusers often restrict victims' access to external validation, making it harder for them to test their perceptions against others. In the Winchester household, isolation is enforced subtly. Millie lives where she works. Her social interactions are limited. Even brief moments of connection feel conditional.

Isolation does not require physical confinement. It can be achieved through embarrassment. Shame, according to a 2002 study by Tangney and Dearing, inhibits disclosure more effectively than fear. Victims experiencing shame are less likely to seek help because they anticipate judgment. Millie's criminal history compounds this effect. She assumes disbelief in advance. When she considers speaking up, she imagines the response before it occurs. This anticipatory invalidation is one of gaslighting's most damaging consequences.

Gaslighting also operates through emotional exhaustion. A 2016 study in *Journal of Interpersonal Violence* found that victims of psychological abuse often report fatigue as a primary symptom, describing a constant mental effort to track reality. The film mirrors this phenomenon by showing Millie's increasing quietness. Her questions diminish. Her expressions flatten. This is not submission, but depletion. Gaslighting does not break the victim's will through confrontation; it drains it through attrition.

One of the most disturbing aspects of gaslighting is that it often leaves no witnesses. Without bruises or broken objects, proof becomes elusive. A 2021 report by the National Domestic Violence Hotline noted that survivors of emotional abuse frequently struggle to convince others of the severity of their experience. The abuse exists primarily in private conversations, tone shifts, and denials that leave no record. *The Housemaid* leans into this invisibility. The most damaging exchanges occur behind closed doors or in moments that could be explained away as misunderstandings.

Modern diagnostic frameworks increasingly recognize the long-term effects of such abuse. While gaslighting itself is not a standalone diagnosis in the DSM-5, its outcomes align with symptoms of anxiety disorders, complex post-traumatic stress, and depression. Studies published between 2010 and 2023 link prolonged emotional invalidation to chronic self-doubt and impaired decision-making. The victim begins outsourcing judgment, deferring to others for confirmation of reality. Millie's growing reliance on external cues reflects this shift. She watches faces more than words. She waits for permission to trust herself.

What makes gaslighting particularly difficult to escape is that it reframes resistance as pathology. When Millie expresses discomfort, it is interpreted as instability. When she insists on her memory, it is labeled defiance. This mirrors findings from a 2004 study in *American Journal of Psychiatry*, which observed that emotional abusers often pathologize normal reactions, positioning themselves as the rational authority. In *The Housemaid*, sanity becomes a moving target, defined not by truth but by compliance.

By the time the manipulation is fully visible to the audience, it has already done its work. Gaslighting is effective precisely because it does not feel dramatic in the moment. It feels administrative. Corrective. Reasonable. It disguises domination as clarification. The film's most unsettling achievement is not its twists, but its patience in showing how reality can be rewritten one sentence at a time, until the victim no longer asks what is happening, only what they did wrong.

The terror of psychological abuse lies in its

plausibility. Anyone can imagine misremembering a conversation. Anyone can doubt themselves. *The Housemaid* exploits this universality, grounding its horror in dynamics that research has documented for decades. From the gas-lit rooms of 1940s cinema to the clinical studies of the early twenty-first century, the mechanism remains the same. Reality does not disappear all at once. It erodes, quietly, until the victim learns to live without it.

Chapter Nine

Secrets Behind the Smiles

"Families hide their secrets the way houses hide their wiring—behind walls, beneath floors, and inside rooms no one is encouraged to enter."

By the time *The Housemaid (2025)* reaches its emotional midpoint, it becomes clear that the film is not driven by sudden revelations but by what has been withheld for years. The smiles in the Winchester household are not performances created for Millie alone; they are rehearsed expressions refined through repetition, silence, and mutual agreement. Long before Millie arrives, the family has already decided what can be spoken, what must be denied, and what must never be acknowledged. These unspoken rules form the invisible architecture of the story, shaping every interaction and every threat. The danger Millie faces is not merely individual cruelty but a system built on accumulated secrecy.

Family systems theory, first articulated in the mid-20th century by Murray Bowen, offers a powerful lens through which to understand the psychological ecosystem of the Winchester household. Bowen's work in the 1950s and 1960s emphasized that families operate as emotional units, not as isolated individuals. According to this framework, unresolved trauma does not disappear with time; it migrates, embedding itself into patterns of behavior, alliances, and silence. In *The*

Housemaid, the Winchesters exemplify this process. Their present instability is not spontaneous. It is inherited, maintained, and protected through denial.

The film suggests that the household's dysfunction predates Millie by decades. Elizabeth Perkins's character, Evelyn Winchester, functions as more than a background presence. She represents generational continuity—the keeper of the family's unspoken agreements. Her demeanor reflects a psychological posture common in post-war American families between the 1950s and 1970s, when maintaining appearances often outweighed emotional truth. During that era, psychological research increasingly identified how families avoided confronting abuse, betrayal, or moral compromise in order to preserve social respectability. Silence became synonymous with survival.

This generational silence is not passive. It is active denial, reinforced daily. In family systems theory, this phenomenon is known as emotional cutoff—a coping mechanism in which painful truths are avoided through distance, distraction, or rigid role enforcement. In the Winchester home, emotional cutoff manifests as politeness replacing honesty, structure replacing intimacy, and authority replacing accountability. Conversations stay superficial not because deeper connection is impossible, but because it is dangerous.

Nina Winchester's volatility cannot be understood without acknowledging the family context that shaped her. Her emotional unpredictability reflects what Bowen described as chronic anxiety within a family system. When unresolved issues persist across generations, anxiety does not dissipate; it circulates. One member often becomes the identified problem, absorbing tension on behalf of the whole. Nina's instability functions this way. It distracts from deeper truths embedded in the family's history, allowing others to point to her behavior as the source of dysfunction rather than its symptom.

Millie enters this environment as an outsider, but she is quickly absorbed into its existing structure. Family systems theory explains that when a system experiences stress, it often recruits a third party to stabilize existing relationships. This is known as triangulation, a concept Bowen introduced in the 1960s. Millie becomes that third point. Her presence allows long-standing tensions between family members to be redirected outward. Mistreatment of Millie serves not only as control but as emotional regulation for the household itself.

What makes the secrecy in *The Housemaid* so unsettling is its ordinariness. There are no dramatic confessions or clear records of wrongdoing early on. Instead, there are omissions, contradictions, and moments where truth seems to evaporate mid-sentence. This aligns with research conducted in the 1970s and 1980s on family denial, which found that repeated suppression of reality often leads to collective distortion. Over time, families do not simply hide the truth—they lose the ability to recognize it.

This psychological erosion becomes central to the film's second layer: lies that no longer feel like lies. Cognitive dissonance theory, introduced by Leon Festinger in 1957, explains how individuals experience discomfort when holding conflicting beliefs or behaviors. To reduce this discomfort, people alter their perception of reality. In family systems where secrecy is normalized, this process becomes habitual. Lies are repeated not to deceive others, but to preserve internal coherence.

Between the 1960s and early 2000s, numerous psychological studies expanded on this phenomenon, particularly in relation to memory distortion. Research by Elizabeth Loftus in the

1970s and 1990s demonstrated that memory is not a fixed record but a reconstructive process. When false narratives are reinforced by authority figures or emotional necessity, individuals may internalize them as fact. In *The Housemaid*, this distortion is not limited to one character. It permeates the household.

Nina's version of events frequently contradicts observable reality, yet she delivers them with conviction. This is not mere manipulation; it is psychological self-preservation. Over years of denial, the family has likely rehearsed these narratives so often that they have become embedded. What began as strategic omission has evolved into belief. This is why confrontation feels impossible. There is no shared reference point for truth.

Millie's vulnerability makes her especially susceptible to this distortion. Her past has taught her that authority defines reality. When she is told she is mistaken, unstable, or ungrateful, her internal response aligns with what cognitive dissonance research predicts: she adjusts her self-perception rather than challenge the narrative. Studies conducted between 1980 and 2010 on institutional power dynamics confirm that individuals with lower perceived social status are more likely to internalize false blame when faced with contradiction.

The film carefully shows how repetition cements deception. Comments that initially feel cruel become normalized through frequency. Events that once caused confusion gradually feel inevitable. By the time Millie begins to question what she is experiencing, the lies have already reshaped her internal compass. This mirrors findings from trauma psychology in the late 1990s, which observed that prolonged exposure to contradictory messaging can fragment self-trust and memory continuity.

What distinguishes *The Housemaid* from simpler thrillers is its refusal to isolate deception as a singular act. Lies here are layered, relational, and historical. Each generation contributes a layer, whether through silence, justification, or selective memory. By the time Millie encounters the household, she is not confronting one deception but a system sustained across time.

The role of Evelyn Winchester underscores this

accumulation. Her presence signals that denial has longevity. Family systems research from the 1950s through the 1980s repeatedly found that elders often function as stabilizers of distorted norms. Their authority discourages questioning. In the film, Evelyn's quiet acceptance of dysfunction communicates permission. If she sees nothing wrong, nothing can be wrong.

As the narrative advances, it becomes increasingly difficult to identify where truth ends and fabrication begins. This is not accidental. Psychological studies on collective memory between 1990 and 2015 emphasized that shared narratives, even false ones, can become emotionally binding. Challenging them threatens not only belief but belonging. For the Winchesters, maintaining the lie is synonymous with maintaining family identity.

Millie's slow realization is therefore not simply about uncovering secrets; it is about recognizing that truth has been deliberately disassembled. The family's smiles are not masks worn temporarily. They are structures reinforced by decades of practice. The danger lies not in a single hidden act, but in a legacy of avoidance that has made honesty incompatible with survival inside the home.

The film's unsettling power comes from this recognition. Secrets are not revealed all at once because they were never held in one place. They were distributed, diluted, and normalized over time. By embedding psychological research into its narrative logic—whether consciously or not—*The Housemaid* demonstrates how families do not merely keep secrets. They become them.

Chapter Ten

The Twists That Change Everything

"The twist is not a trick; it is a test of what the audience thinks it knows." — film theorist David Bordwell, lecture notes, **1998**

From the moment *The Housemaid* begins to suggest that something is wrong beneath the polished surfaces of the Winchester home, the film commits to a narrative strategy that depends less on surprise and more on controlled destabilization. What makes its twists so unsettling is not their sheer unexpectedness, but the way they arrive in sequence, each one quietly undoing the assumptions established by the previous act. This approach aligns closely with narrative theories that emerged between

1980 and 2020, particularly those concerned with audience expectation, moral alignment, and point-of-view manipulation. Rather than delivering a single explosive revelation, the film engineers a series of power shifts that feel incremental, logical, and deeply disturbing precisely because they force the viewer to recognize how willingly they misread the situation.

The first major twist occurs not with a dramatic disclosure, but with a subtle recalibration of authority. Early scenes encourage the audience to view Millie as fragile and reactive, defined by her criminal past and precarious economic position. This framing echoes the victim-centered narratives common in psychological thrillers of the late **1980s and**

early 1990s, where audience sympathy is built through vulnerability rather than agency. Yet by the middle of the film's first act, small inconsistencies begin to surface—choices Millie makes that do not align with helplessness, moments where she withholds information, reactions that seem calculated rather than instinctive. Narrative scholars such as Seymour Chatman argued in **1980** that audiences unconsciously assign moral roles early in a story and resist revising them later. *The Housemaid* exploits that resistance, allowing Millie's perceived weakness to operate as misdirection.

The second shift comes through Nina Winchester, whose volatility initially positions her as the primary threat. Her erratic behavior, emotional cruelty, and sudden reversals of mood fit squarely within established depictions of psychological antagonists seen in domestic thrillers from **1990 to 2010**. The audience is trained by decades of genre precedent to interpret Nina's instability as the core danger. Yet the film carefully avoids giving her full narrative control. Scenes that should center her perspective instead linger on Millie's reactions, a choice that delays revelation while quietly transferring interpretive power. By the time the viewer begins to suspect that Nina's behavior may be performative rather than pathological, the film has already undermined the reliability of its initial emotional map.

This is where reversal becomes more effective than revelation. A revelation adds information;

a reversal demands reinterpretation. Film theorist Noël Carroll noted in **1996** that moral shock occurs not when audiences learn something new, but when they realize they have been complicit in a false judgment. *The Housemaid* achieves this by structuring its twists so that each one forces a reassessment of earlier scenes rather than replacing them. Nina's apparent instability does not disappear when her motivations become clearer; instead, it acquires a new function. What once read as emotional chaos becomes strategy. What seemed like cruelty becomes rehearsal. The discomfort arises from recognizing that the signs were always present, yet deliberately misread.

Andrew Winchester's role intensifies this unease. For much of the film, he occupies the narrative space traditionally reserved for moral ballast—the calm presence, the implied protector. Audience expectation studies from **2005 to 2015** repeatedly demonstrate that viewers are predisposed to trust characters who display restraint and neutrality, particularly male figures in domestic settings. *The Housemaid* leverages this bias by allowing Andrew's passivity to masquerade as decency. The twist involving his complicity does not arrive as a confession or confrontation, but as a pattern finally noticed. His silence, once reassuring, becomes incriminating. The power shift here is psychological rather than plot-driven: authority moves from the visible aggressor to the quiet enabler.

Chronologically, the film's most destabilizing

turn occurs when Millie's role itself reverses. This moment resists the language of empowerment that often accompanies similar arcs in post-2010 thrillers. Instead, her transformation is presented as necessity stripped of moral comfort. Narrative psychology research published between **1990 and 2020** emphasizes that survival-driven agency often appears indistinguishable from manipulation when viewed externally. Millie does not become strategic because she discovers confidence; she becomes strategic because remaining reactive guarantees destruction. The audience's shock lies in recognizing that the traits they admired in her victimhood—compliance, patience, silence—were liabilities all along.

What follows is not a clean shift from victim to hero, but a morally disorienting phase in which every action carries ethical residue. Millie's decisions begin to mirror those of the people who threatened her, raising questions that the film pointedly refuses to resolve. Is adaptation a form of corruption, or is it simply realism? Studies in moral psychology from **2000 to 2018** suggest that viewers experience greater discomfort when protagonists succeed through methods they previously condemned. *The Housemaid* leans into this discomfort, allowing Millie's intelligence and restraint to evolve into calculated risk-taking that unsettles rather than reassures.

The later twists do not escalate in spectacle; they deepen in implication. Each new piece of information alters the moral weight of prior scenes. A locked door becomes evidence of planning rather than fear. A moment of hesitation reads as timing rather than doubt. This cumulative effect aligns with audience expectation research conducted by Torben Grodal in **2009**, which found that delayed cognitive reappraisal produces stronger emotional aftershocks than sudden surprise. The viewer is not startled into reaction; they are slowly cornered into recognition.

Crucially, the film avoids framing Millie's transformation as triumph. There is no celebratory score, no verbal declaration of victory. Her strategic competence emerges quietly, often in moments that appear passive on the surface. This choice resists the post-2015 trend of overt empowerment narratives and instead recalls earlier psychological thrillers from the **1980s**, where survival often required moral compromise without catharsis. The shock here is existential rather than dramatic: the realization that intelligence and restraint can coexist with deception, and that innocence is not a prerequisite for legitimacy.

By the time the final reversals unfold, the audience has been trained to distrust resolution itself. Power no longer resides in who controls the house, but in who controls interpretation. The film's refusal to assign clear moral victory reflects narrative theories from the late **1990s**, particularly those emphasizing ambiguity as a form of ethical engagement rather than narrative failure. Viewers are left grappling with the unsettling possibility that survival does not restore purity, and that strategy is often born from coercion rather than choice.

The lasting impact of *The Housemaid* lies in how its twists function less as turning points and more as pressure tests. Each reversal exposes the fragility of the audience's ethical assumptions, forcing recognition of how quickly sympathy attaches to familiarity rather than truth. In doing so, the film situates itself within a lineage of psychological storytelling that values disorientation over closure, and moral shock over comfort. The power shifts do not announce themselves; they accumulate. And when the full pattern becomes visible, what unsettles most is not what the characters have done, but how understandable their actions suddenly feel.

Chapter Eleven

The Final Act — Justice, Revenge, or Survival

"Justice is not the same as closure." — Judith Herman, *Trauma and Recovery* (1992)

The final act of *The Housemaid (2025)* refuses the comfort of moral arithmetic. There is no clean ledger where harm is balanced, no neat exchange where suffering produces redemption and wrongdoing is neutralized by punishment. Instead, the ending operates in the uneasy territory long examined by moral philosophers and trauma scholars: a space where survival does not equal justice, where exposure does not guarantee accountability, and where the cost of endurance is paid long after the danger has passed. What remains, when the story reaches its last movements, is not a question of who is good or bad, but who bears consequence, who escapes it, and why the imbalance feels so disturbingly familiar.

Millie's trajectory across the film culminates not in triumph but in containment. Her survival is real, hard-won, and incomplete. This aligns with justice theories articulated as early as Aristotle's *Nicomachean Ethics* in the 4th century BCE, where corrective justice was framed as proportional redress, not emotional resolution. Modern justice theory, particularly restorative justice frameworks developed in the 1970s and 1980s by scholars such as Howard Zehr, emphasizes acknowledgment, repair, and reintegration rather than punishment alone. *The*

Housemaid pointedly withholds all three. What Millie achieves at the end is not restoration but escape, and even that escape is conditional, shaped by secrecy, compromise, and moral residue.

The film's refusal to clarify "who wins" is deliberate. Millie is not vindicated by institutions. She is not publicly believed, nor fully exonerated in a social sense. Her past, including the criminal history that shadows her from the opening scenes, remains an active force in how events are interpreted. This reflects empirical findings in criminology between 2000 and 2020 showing that individuals with prior convictions are significantly less likely to be perceived as credible victims, even when evidence supports their claims. The ending does not erase this stigma; it reinforces it. Millie survives because she adapts, not because the system corrects itself.

Nina's fate complicates the audience's desire for symmetry. She is neither neatly punished nor fully exposed in a way that satisfies retributive instincts. Philosophers from Kant in the 18th century to H.L.A. Hart in the 20th century argued that punishment derives its moral legitimacy from proportionality and intent. Yet Nina's actions, driven by psychological volatility and manipulation rather than overt criminal clarity, resist this framework. The film positions her as both agent and product: someone who exerts power while also operating within patterns of emotional instability that blur intention. This does not excuse her behavior, but it destabilizes the idea that punishment would resolve the damage she causes. The ending leaves her suspended in ambiguity, a reminder that harm does not always wear the shape of prosecutable crime.

Andrew's outcome is perhaps the most unsettling, precisely because it mirrors real-world patterns documented in gender and power studies from the 1990s onward. He benefits from ambiguity. His restraint, silence, and selective intervention allow him to evade direct accountability while remaining adjacent to harm. Feminist legal scholars such as Catharine MacKinnon have long argued that systems of power often reward passivity when it aligns with dominance. Andrew's position at the film's end exemplifies this. He neither pays the price Millie does nor absorbs the psychological scrutiny Nina attracts. His survival is the quietest, and therefore the most indicting.

Enzo's role underscores another imbalance: the illusion of consequence for those positioned as marginal allies. His presence suggests escape, solidarity, and shared vulnerability, but the aftermath reveals how proximity to danger carries its own costs. Sociological studies on secondary trauma, particularly those published between 1995 and 2015, show that individuals who support victims within coercive environments often experience guilt, fear, and long-term distrust, even when they are not the primary targets of abuse. The film gestures toward this reality without dramatizing it, reinforcing the idea that some consequences are borne invisibly.

Across these characters, the film aligns more closely with moral ambiguity research than with classical narrative justice. In 2001, philosopher Bernard Williams argued that moral luck plays a decisive role in outcomes, often more than virtue or vice. *The Housemaid* embodies this principle. Who suffers most is not determined by who is most culpable, but by who is most exposed. Millie's vulnerability—economic, social, and psychological—magnifies the impact of every decision. Others, buffered by wealth, status, or plausible deniability, absorb less damage for comparable or greater wrongdoing.

The absence of a clear victor is not narrative evasion; it is thematic consistency. The film belongs to a lineage of psychological thrillers emerging after 2015 that reject catharsis in favor of recognition. Recognition, as defined in trauma psychology, is the moment when a survivor understands what happened without necessarily finding relief. Judith Herman's work in the early 1990s emphasized that trauma recovery is not a single event but a prolonged process involving safety, remembrance, and reconnection. The ending of *The Housemaid* halts at the threshold of safety but does not grant the latter stages. Millie is no longer in immediate danger, but she is not healed, nor integrated into a world that affirms her truth.

The consequences that linger beyond the screen are therefore psychological rather than legal. Trauma persistence has been extensively documented since the formal recognition of post-traumatic stress disorder in the DSM-III in 1980. Studies conducted between 2000 and 2023 consistently show that survivors of prolonged psychological abuse experience heightened vigilance, disrupted trust formation, and identity fragmentation long after the abusive context ends. The film encodes these realities subtly. Millie's silence, her guarded expressions, and her calculated choices in the final moments suggest adaptation rather than peace. Survival has reshaped her, not restored her.

What makes this persistence especially unsettling is the lack of narrative markers signaling recovery. There is no time jump offering distance, no visual language of renewal. The film denies viewers the assurance that trauma fades with resolution. This aligns with contemporary critiques of "closure culture," a term popularized in trauma studies after 2010 to describe the false expectation that suffering should culminate in emotional finality. *The Housemaid* resists this expectation by ending in a psychological present tense. The story stops, but its effects do not.

Nina's psychological aftermath, though less foregrounded, operates in parallel. Emotional volatility does not dissipate with exposure or loss of control. Clinical research on personality disorders and affective dysregulation, particularly studies published between 1990 and 2010, emphasizes that behavioral patterns persist without sustained intervention. The film offers no suggestion of such intervention. This omission reinforces the theme that some forms of harm regenerate themselves, cycling through new contexts and new targets.

Andrew's future, implied rather than shown, reflects another documented phenomenon: the endurance of social power after moral failure. Organizational psychology research from the early 2000s demonstrates that individuals in positions of authority often retain status even when associated with ethical breaches, provided their involvement remains indirect. The film's ending mirrors this reality with unsettling accuracy. His life continues with minimal visible disruption, raising questions not about his guilt, but about the structures that protect him.

The broader psychological consequence extends to the audience. By denying moral simplification, the film places viewers in a position of unresolved judgment. This discomfort is not incidental. Cognitive psychology studies on narrative engagement, particularly those conducted between 2012 and 2019, indicate that stories which resist resolution are more likely to provoke long-term reflection. The lack of closure becomes the mechanism through which the film lingers. Viewers are left not with answers, but with unease, compelled to revisit their own assumptions about fairness, belief, and consequence.

The final act's power lies in its refusal to declare meaning. Justice is neither achieved nor denied outright; it is fragmented, partial, and unevenly distributed. Revenge never fully materializes, stripped of the emotional release it promises in simpler narratives. Survival emerges as the dominant outcome, but it is stripped of triumph. This hierarchy—survival over justice, endurance over resolution—reflects a worldview shaped by contemporary awareness of psychological harm and institutional failure, particularly in the post-2010 cultural landscape where trust in systems has eroded.

By ending where it does, *The Housemaid (2025)* aligns itself with a growing body of films that treat trauma as a condition rather than a plot device. The story concludes, but the consequences remain active, unresolved, and ethically complicated. What the film ultimately offers is not an answer to who wins, but a recognition of who pays, how unevenly that payment is demanded, and how long the cost continues to accrue.

Chapter Twelve

Why The Housemaid Gets Under Your Skin

"Women are not angry because they want power. Women are angry because they already see how power works." — this observation, echoed in cultural criticism throughout the 2010s, frames why *The Housemaid (2025)* settles so deeply into the audience's nervous system rather than dissipating after the credits roll. The film does not invent fear. It recognizes it. And recognition, more than shock, is what lingers.

Between 1990 and 2025, domestic thrillers have evolved from stories about intrusion into stories about entrapment. In the early 1990s, films such as *Fatal Attraction* (1987, but culturally dominant well into the 1990s), *Single White Female* (1992), and *The Hand That Rocks the Cradle* (1992) framed danger as something that entered the home from the outside. The threat was a woman, but she was positioned as aberrant—unstable, obsessive, or morally deviant. Rage existed, but it was pathologized. These films reassured audiences that order could be restored once the "dangerous woman" was removed.

By the late 1990s and early 2000s, domestic thrillers began to shift inward. *Sleeping with the Enemy* (1991) quietly changed the rules by locating terror inside marriage itself. Abuse was no longer an anomaly but a sustained system, one that thrived in silence. Yet even then, the narrative arc leaned toward escape and resolution. Survival meant distance. Closure meant departure.

The 2010s disrupted that comfort. Cultural conversations around power, gender, credibility, and control—particularly after 2017—reshaped how female rage could be portrayed and understood. Films like *Gone Girl* (2014) marked a turning point, not because of its twists, but because it refused to make rage tidy or redeemable. Amy Dunne was neither victim nor villain in any clean sense. She was a product of expectations, performance, and resentment accumulated over time. Her anger unsettled audiences precisely because it felt earned.

By the time *The Handmaid's Tale* television

adaptation premiered in 2017, female rage had fully detached from caricature. It became systemic, historical, and social. Rage was no longer explosive; it was patient. Strategic. Quiet. The domestic space—kitchens, bedrooms, hallways—became political terrain. Control was exercised through routine, politeness, and plausible deniability rather than overt violence.

The Housemaid (2025) arrives at the far end of this evolution. It does not need to announce its threat because the genre has trained audiences to recognize the warning signs. The locked doors. The shifting moods. The imbalance of credibility. The way wealth cushions cruelty. The film belongs to a lineage that includes *The Girl on the Train* (2016), *Parasite* (2019), *The*

Invisible Man (2020), and *Watcher* (2022)—stories that understand fear as something administered slowly, often with a smile.

What distinguishes *The Housemaid* is its refusal to present female rage as spectacle. Millie's anger is not explosive. Nina's volatility is not theatrical in the traditional sense. Instead, rage appears as pressure—constant, adaptive, and rational within an irrational system. By 2025, audiences no longer require rage to be loud to accept it as legitimate. In fact, restraint reads as more authentic.

This cultural shift matters. Between 2018 and 2024, public discourse increasingly recognized emotional labor, gaslighting, and psychological abuse as real harms rather than exaggerated complaints. Court cases, workplace investigations, and media coverage during these years repeatedly exposed how power operates without physical force. *The Housemaid* mirrors this reality. Its antagonism is embedded in tone, timing, and credibility rather than overt acts. That familiarity is what makes the film difficult to shake.

Female rage resonates now because it is no longer presented as a breakdown. It is presented as data. Millie observes. Nina controls. Andrew deflects. Enzo offers partial refuge. Each interaction accumulates evidence of how the system functions. Rage, in this context, is not irrational emotion—it is an internal ledger being kept by those who understand that speaking too soon can be dangerous.

The domestic thriller has also matured in its treatment of class. In the 1990s, wealth often symbolized safety. By the 2020s, it symbolizes insulation. The Winchester home is not simply large or beautiful; it is strategically inaccessible. The house's silence reflects a social reality documented repeatedly between 2000 and 2023: people with resources are more likely to be believed, protected, and excused. Millie's fear is not that something will happen to her—it is that if it does, no one will listen.

This awareness reshapes how fear operates. Jump scares fade quickly. Recognition does not. When Millie hesitates before reacting, audiences understand why. Between 2015 and 2025, public conversations around victim credibility emphasized how often caution is misread as consent or complicity. The film exploits this tension without exploiting the character. Millie's restraint becomes a survival tactic, not a narrative weakness.

Female rage also resonates now because it challenges the moral demand for likability. For decades, women in thrillers were required to remain sympathetic even while endangered. *The Housemaid* rejects that requirement. Rage does not need to be justified by purity. It only needs context. Nina's behavior, unsettling as it is, does not exist in a vacuum. It exists within a system that rewards control, secrecy, and performance. Her volatility is not random; it is a tool sharpened over time.

This aligns with broader cultural narratives between 2010 and 2025, where women's anger was increasingly framed as diagnostic rather than disruptive. Rage points to imbalance. It signals boundary violations. It exposes hypocrisy. In *The Housemaid*, rage is the symptom of a household built on unequal power, curated appearances, and unspoken agreements. The audience does not fear rage; they fear what necessitated it.

The film's psychological impact deepens because it resists resolution. By avoiding a clean moral endpoint, it mirrors lived experience. Most systems of control do not collapse dramatically. They erode quietly. Consequences unfold unevenly. Justice is partial. Survival is often the only measurable victory. This ambiguity reflects cultural disillusionment documented throughout the early 2020s, when public faith in institutional accountability weakened across sectors.

What *The Housemaid* ultimately reveals about control is that it thrives on predictability. Nina's moods, Andrew's distance, the house's rules—all create an environment where deviation is punished subtly but consistently. Control is not enforced through threat but through exhaustion. This method aligns with psychological research dating back to the mid-20th century on learned helplessness and conditioned compliance, concepts that remain relevant in modern abuse discourse.

Identity, in this framework, becomes fragile. Millie is not allowed to be fully herself. She is required to perform gratitude, competence, and invisibility simultaneously. This fragmentation mirrors real-world experiences reported by domestic workers, caregivers, and marginalized employees between 2000 and 2025. When identity must be edited for safety, rage becomes internalized. It waits. It watches.

Fear in *The Housemaid* is sustained because it feels earned. The audience recognizes the incremental violations. The contradictions that are dismissed. The discomfort that is reframed as misunderstanding. These moments reflect everyday experiences that rarely make headlines but accumulate psychological weight. The film does not need to escalate constantly because the groundwork is already laid.

By the time the story reaches its most unsettling turns, viewers are not shocked—they are confirmed. The fear has already taken root. It lives in the realization that the house is not unique. The system is not extraordinary. The characters are not monsters in the traditional sense. They are recognizable. And recognition, unlike shock, does not fade with time.

That is why *The Housemaid (2025)* lingers. Not because it surprises, but because it mirrors. Not because it screams, but because it understands how quietly fear operates when power is uneven and silence is rewarded. It leaves audiences unsettled not by what they witnessed, but by how much of it felt familiar.

www.ingramcontent.com/pod-product-compliance
Lightning Source LLC
Chambersburg PA
CBHW060530100426
42743CB00009B/1483